Outrageously Adorable

dog knits

Outrageously Adorable
dog knits

25 Must-Have Styles for the Pampered Pooch

Featuring knits by Jill Bulgan, Noelle Woosley,
Rachael Matthews, and Max Alexander

Race Point
PUBLISHING

Dedicated to Ivy, Poppy, Tilly, Percy, Ruby, Jade, Casper, Elmo, Coco, Carla, Schnitzel, and Harry Potter. Thanks for the sniffs and licks.

Race Point Publishing
An imprint of Quarto Publishing Group USA Inc.
276 Fifth Avenue, Suite 205
New York, New York 10001

RACE POINT PUBLISHING and the distinctive Race Point Publishing
logo are trademarks of Quarto Publishing Group USA Inc.

Jill Bulgan is the creator and author of the following patterns: Vintage Ruffled Bonnet, French Beret, Ten-Gallon Cowboy Hat, Toasty Legwarmers, Sports Fanatic Bobble Hat and Scarf, Personalized Doggie Blanket, Cupcake Skirt and Hat, Trendy Cowl, Cutesy Booties, Chic Shawl.

Noelle Woosley is the creator and author of the following patterns: Elizabethan Ruff, Feelin' Fancy Bowtie, Pompom Scarf for Petite Pooches, Chunky Scarf for the Larger Dog, Simple Roll-Neck Pullover, Holiday Patterned Sweater, Preppy Puppy Letterman Sweater, Rabbit-Ear Bonnet, Urban Hoodie, Stylish Stripes Sweater, Elf Hat, Rose Corsage.

Rachael Matthews and Max Alexander are the the creators and authors of the following patterns: Bumblebee Costume, Superhero Cape and Wristbands.

Text by Caitlin Doyle.

Getting Started by Gemma Birss.

ISBN 978-1-631060-43-4

Printed and bound in China

10 9 8 7 6 5 4 3 2 1

www.racepointpub.com

Cover and interior photography by Claire Lloyd Davies

No dogs were harmed or humiliated in the making of this book.

contents

introduction/author's note

Have you ever been all dressed up with no place to go? Well, imagine having the whole world at your (four) feet, but not a stitch to wear! Never fear; this book removes that bane of shame for your loyal best friend.

Your pooch adores you and has gone to so much trouble to show it. Just consider all that work Max put into chewing your slippers just *so* to ensure they epitomize worn-in comfort. Or the energy Bella has expended in growling away the mailman to keep unwanted bills at bay. It's time to return their gallant efforts. And what says "I love you" better than a flashy, one-of-a-kind superhero costume for patrolling the house? Or a hand-knit holiday sweater to complement the family photos on Christmas morning against a backdrop of shredded wrapping, courtesy of Olive the puppy?

Amusement is mutual: our pawed pals delight us, as we must surely fascinate them with our strange behaviors, such as relegating perfectly decent "trash" to a can and greeting the wrong end of fellow humans. However, of course, not all dogs like to be paraded for our entertainment. But some simply revel in the attention. If your pampered pup is one of the latter, you'll be all too familiar with the signs:

lapping up the limelight at every dinner party; showing off tricks to each and every new guest; leaving you in a heartbeat if a more captivating lap becomes available; posing perfectly at the first sign of a camera phone. If you share your home with such a diva, get some knitting needles *pronto* and start crafting some haute couture duds for your little angel.

Do remember that, like humans, dogs have their individual likes and dislikes. Some seem to love a good dress-up—even if it's at the grasping hands of an enthusiastic toddler. But others may have delicate ears, a sensitive paw, a strong aversion to wearing hats . . . or perhaps a more finely tuned fashion palate than yours. *Don't push it.* We love our fur kids, and our job as their keepers is to ensure that they're happy and healthy. So, before embarking on a time-consuming display of affection by knitting Milo an intricate cowboy hat, first test out whether he minds having his head adorned. If he is happily behatted, knit away! If he's not, perhaps choose some other delightful apparel to express your adoration. We employed the same caveat during our photo shoot—*please rest assured, no dogs were harmed or humiliated in the making of this book.*

Once you've ascertained your pet's style preferences, it's time to start knitting. This book will guide you to create bespoke knitwear for your cherished pooch—as well as setting you merrily on your way to developing your own designs. For novice knitters, simple patterns are clearly marked, while further embellishments and more complex outfits ensure that experienced woolsmiths are catered for, too. Most items can be tweaked to fit dogs of any size and shape—simply follow the individual pattern's measurement instructions. However, some garments are less straightforward and, as such, come in a one-size-fits-most format. Please consider your dog's statistics carefully before beginning a project.

The designs in this book have been carefully chosen to accommodate all levels, with a range of knitwear options, from fun Halloween costumes, to everyday sweaters for snuggling up in front of the fire on a cold winter's night, and everything in between. The wonderful knitters involved in this project come from a variety of backgrounds, but every one is passionate about sharing the joy of their craft and creating unique and wearable designs. Please read more about them in the Contributors section on p. 95 and check out their websites for more inspiration.

So, get those needles clacking and prepare to be showered with praise for your fine crafting skills and your pet's dashing outfits. Enjoy your knitting adventure!

Dogs can't knit. But they sure can wear it well.

getting started

MAKE A SLIPKNOT

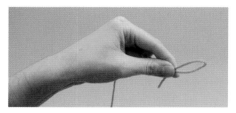

1 Cross the yarn into a loop and pinch closed
with your thumb and forefinger, holding the
short end of the yarn underneath.

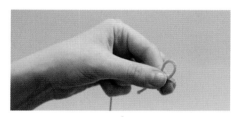

2 With the longer yarn length, make a second loop
over and around the tip of your forefinger.

3 Pull the second loop through the first.

CASTING ON

1 Hold a needle in your left hand and tighten the
slipknot around it. This is your first stitch.

2 Insert the right-hand needle into the stitch,
crossing it behind the left needle. Loop the yarn
behind and around the right needle.

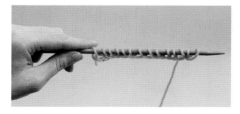

3 Draw the right needle under the left needle, catching the
loop and transferring it across. You have created your
second stitch. Continue until you have a row of stitches.

KNIT STITCH

1 Hold the stitched needle in your left hand and the free needle in your right, keeping the yarn at the back of your work. Insert the right-hand needle into the first stitch, crossing behind the left needle.

3 Draw the right needle under the left, catching the loop and transferring it across.

2 Loop the yarn behind and around the right needle.

4 Continue with knit stitch for a more textured finish.

PURL STITCH

1 The technique for purl is similar to knit, but instead of inserting the right needle behind the left in the stitch, you angle it in front. Keep the yarn at the front of the work.

2 Loop the yarn over and around the right needle.

3 Draw the right needle under the left, catching the loop and transferring it across.

4 Purl creates a smoother, flatter finish than knit stitch.

CASTING OFF

1 Keeping the yarn at the back of your work, knit the first two stitches onto the right-hand needle.

2 Insert the left needle into the stitch that's furthest from the tip.

3 Lift this stitch over the other stitch, slipping it off the needle.

4 Knit another stitch onto the right-hand needle and repeat to the end of the row.
5 When there is one stitch left, slip it off the needle and thread the yarn through to secure it.

ABBREVIATIONS

sts—stitches

k—knit

k1—knit one stitch

p—purl

p1—purl one stitch

m1—miss one—i.e., knit into front and back of same stitch

k2tog—knit 2 stitches together

k3tog—knit 3 stitches together

ktbl—knit into the back of the stitch

yo—yarn over—i.e., bring yarn over the needle and back to the front to make a loop

x2—make two

Rib stitch—k1, p1

Garter stitch—knit all rows

Stockinette stitch—knit one row, pearl one row

Seed stitch—2 rows: k1, p1, 2 rows: p1, k1. Repeat continuously

TIPS

- Your pet's skin may be sensitive to wool, so use acrylic yarn where possible

- Keep your stitches relaxed and loose to make life easier

- When adapting the patterns for bigger dogs, use larger needles and chunky yarn

- Have fun with colors and embellishments!

stylish headwear

vintage ruffled bonnet

Inspired by antique Victorian lace bonnets, this beautiful example of hand-knit finery will look darling on furry friends with larger heads (and calmer dispositions). Knit in pure white for an authentic look or choose a bright color or stripes for a wild take on a classic pattern—or go all out with a super-sized rose corsage (see pp. 18–19)!

This was knitted for a dog with a bulldog-shaped-head. The bonnet is worked in one piece from the ties at the back through to the front picot edging. You could embellish it with flowers, beads, buttons, or lace. To adapt it for a smaller dog, use size 2 (2.75mm) knitting needles and 4-ply yarn, or to make it larger, try chunky yarn with size 9 (5.5mm) needles.

MATERIALS

Size 6 (4mm) knitting needles
Double knit yarn
Darning needle

DIRECTIONS

Cast on 130 sts
Knit first 2 rows
On next 2 rows, cast off 50 sts and knit to end
Knit 1 row
Purl 1 row
Continue in stockinette stitch for 21 rows
With the right side facing, cast on 24 sts and knit to end of row
With the wrong side facing, cast on 24 sts and purl to end of row
Continue in stockinette stitch for 16 rows
Knit 2 rows
Purl 1 row
K1, * yo (yarn over), k2tog, repeat from * to last stitch, k1
Purl 1 row
Knit 1 row
Purl 1 row
Cast off knit-wise
Fold under picot edging and sew to underside of bonnet. Sew side seams. Sew bottom side edges to ties, stretching the ties as you sew. Weave in all loose ends

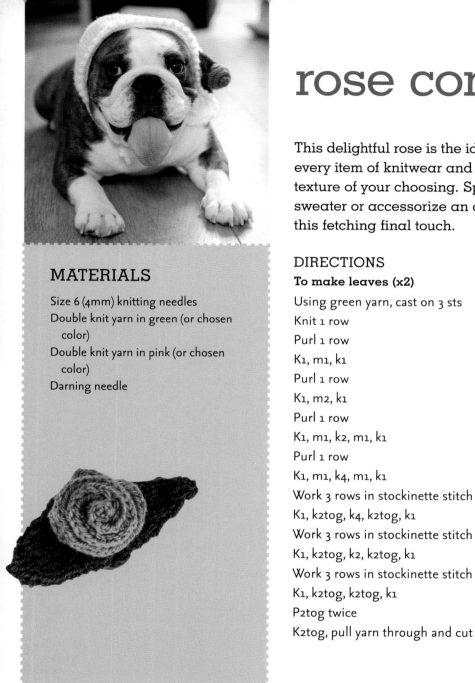

rose corsage

This delightful rose is the ideal embellishment for almost every item of knitwear and can be created in any color or texture of your choosing. Spruce up an everyday roll-neck sweater or accessorize an adorable vintage bonnet with this fetching final touch.

MATERIALS

Size 6 (4mm) knitting needles
Double knit yarn in green (or chosen color)
Double knit yarn in pink (or chosen color)
Darning needle

DIRECTIONS

To make leaves (x2)

Using green yarn, cast on 3 sts
Knit 1 row
Purl 1 row
K1, m1, k1
Purl 1 row
K1, m2, k1
Purl 1 row
K1, m1, k2, m1, k1
Purl 1 row
K1, m1, k4, m1, k1
Work 3 rows in stockinette stitch
K1, k2tog, k4, k2tog, k1
Work 3 rows in stockinette stitch
K1, k2tog, k2, k2tog, k1
Work 3 rows in stockinette stitch
K1, k2tog, k2tog, k1
P2tog twice
K2tog, pull yarn through and cut

To make rose

With pink yarn, cast on 8 sts
Knit in stockinette stitch until piece measures 10 in. (25.5cm)
(For a larger rose, keep knitting until you've reached desired size)
Cast off and weave in any loose ends
Roll up and sew onto leaves

(Note: Ensure that such embellishments are tightly stitched onto knitwear and that chew-prone puppies in particular are supervised when wearing them, as they may present a choking hazard.)

elf hat

Who can resist such an adorable little Christmas elf . . . even when she has just knocked over the tree, yanked down the tinsel, and eaten all the presents?

MATERIALS

Size 6 (4mm) knitting needles
Double knit yarn in green (or chosen color)
Double knit yarn in rust (or chosen color)
Darning needle

DIRECTIONS

To make hat (x2)

Using green yarn, cast on 30 sts
Work in seed stitch for 2 rows
**K2tog, work to last 3 sts, p2tog
Work 1 row**
Repeat from ** to ** until 4 sts remain
K2tog, k2tog
Turn work, k2tog, cut yarn and pull it through
Having made two, put both triangles alongside each other and sew along the two top edges to create a pointed hat, then turn the right way out
Fold in the two pointed edges at bottom of hat and sew them in place along side seam so the bottom edge of the hat is straight

To make trim (x2)

Using rust yarn, cast on 30 sts
Work 3 rows in stockinette stitch, starting and ending with a purl row
On next knit row, **k2tog, k6, k2tog, turn work
Purl back over these 8 sts
Turn, k2tog, k4, k2tog
Purl back over these 6 sts
Turn, k2tog, k2, k2tog
Purl back over these 4 sts
Turn, k2tog twice
P2tog, cut yarn and pull it through**
Returning to remaining 20 sts, repeat from **to** to make three pointed shapes

To make neck band

Using green yarn, cast on 3 sts

Working in garter stitch, work until
piece measures 7 in. (18cm)

It's a good idea to measure under
your dog's chin for a more bespoke
measurement. Remember: the neck
band will stretch

Cast off stitches and weave in
any ends

Using rust yarn, sew the two trims
to the bottom edges of the hat

Using green yarn, sew on the
neck band

French beret

Oh là là! Perfectly adaptable and simply *magnifique* on dogs of all sizes, this beret can be worn at a jaunty angle for Paris chic or as a flat cap for that lovable roguish *je ne sais quoi*. Perfectly paired with a matching shawl (see pp. 46–47), your dog is sure to dazzle as the bark of the town.

This hat was made for Ivy the pug, who measures 4 in. (10cm) between her ears. However, it fits all sizes from pugs to bull mastiffs.

MATERIALS

Size 10½ (6.5mm) knitting needles
Double knit yarn in blue (or chosen color)
Darning needle

DIRECTIONS

Cast on 60 sts

Work first 5 rows in garter stitch (knit each row) to make brim

Increase: k10, *m1 (knit into front and back of same stitch), m1, k1, repeat from * 12 times, then knit last 14 sts

**Purl 1 row

Knit 1 row**

Repeat from ** to ** twice

Purl 1 row

Decrease: *k6, k2tog (knit 2 together), * repeat 10 times, knitting last 4 sts

Purl 1 row

Knit 1 row

Purl 1 row

Decrease: *k5, k2tog, * repeat 10 times, knitting last 4 sts

Purl 1 row

Knit 1 row

Purl 1 row

Decrease: *k4, k2tog, * repeat 10 times, knitting last 4 sts

Purl 1 row

Knit 1 row

Purl 1 row

Decrease: *k3, k2tog, * repeat 10 times, knitting last 4 sts

Purl 1 row

K2tog to end of row

Thread a 3 ft. (1m) length of yarn through all stitches. Turn the beret inside out and pull the loose end through to close the top stitches. Stitch down the back seam and weave in the ends

ten-gallon cowboy hat

They may be little, but they know who's *really* in charge . . . Sheriff Ivy certainly may not look tough, but she commands any lap in her patch and ensures all mailpeople know the rules of the house—if they even dare to approach.

This stetson was knitted for a dog with a span of 4 in. (10cm) between the ears (but it is a one-size-fits-most pattern). It is designed in several sections that are constructed together by knitting the top, adding the main piece, and then finally the brim and tie. Additional features could be sewn on in a contrasting color. The hat is constructed as you knit it.

MATERIALS

Size 6 (4mm) knitting needles
Double knit (DK) yarn
Darning needle

DIRECTIONS

To make top

Cast on 18 sts

Knit the first 4 rows

M1, knit to last stitch, m1

Knit 2 rows

M1, knit to last stitch, m1

Knit 4 rows

M1, knit to last stitch, m1

Knit 3 rows

K2tog, knit to last 2 sts, k2tog

Knit 1 row

K2tog, knit to last 2 sts, k2tog

Knit 4 rows

K2tog, knit to last 2 sts, k2tog

Knit 1 row

M1, knit to last stitch, m1

Knit 1 row

K2tog, knit to last 2 sts, k2tog

End last row with m1 twice

Cast off last 2 sts; this is the back of the top of the hat. Leave a long piece of yarn to sew to the main piece

To make main piece

Cast on 18 sts

Knit as though you were making a scarf, sewing the edge to the circumference of the top part as you go

Start at the back, work around, and end at the back. Join the edges of the main piece together and sew along the back seam

With a new piece of yarn, stitch from the back seam around the edge of the top where it meets the main piece. Use blanket stitch for the detail. To do blanket stitch, loop the thread over as you sew for a decorative edge. This can also be done in a contrasting color

Finally, fold under 2 in. (5cm) of the main piece and sew inside to firm up the main piece

To make brim

Cast on 12 sts

Knit a strip join at the back of the main piece, continuing to sew it to the folded-under edge as you go. Sew it on loosely but stitch the pieces quite close together to ensure it stays in place

To make tie

Knit a 3 ft. (1m) strip by casting on then casting off all stitches

Fold up the brim at each side and attach to the main piece with a couple of stitches. Add the tie by sewing each end under the brim and folding the loop at the bottom to make a knot. Weave in loose ends

(Note: While cute on its own, the cowboy hat can be further embellished with a sheriff badge or other customizations of your choosing. Check out toy stores and eBay for great decorations!)

loungin' around the house

toasty legwarmers

With not a hint of jazzercise in sight, these fun and cozy legwarmers are a tribute to the *Flashdancer* in us all, even if for Tilly that tribute is spent hogging the cushions and snuggling in front of the fire. Pair them with a super-cute matching cowl (see pp. 44–45) for the ultimate cold weather ensemble.

These cozy knits were made for Jade the grayhound, who has a front leg height of 18 in. (46cm), back leg height of 21 in. (53cm), and a circumference each of 5 in. (13cm). They can easily be adjusted for other dogs. Using the front leg length as your starting point, simply doctor the size by reducing or increasing by four stitches for every inch you wish to adjust. The pattern will work over this repeat of stitches.

MATERIALS

Size 10½ (6.5mm) knitting needles
Chunky yarn in pink (or chosen color)
Darning needle

DIRECTIONS

To make front legs (x2)

Cast on 23 sts

For first 4 rows, work in rib (k1,p1) to end of row

Increase: P2, increase in next stitch *p5 increase in next stitch * repeat 3 times, p2 to make 27 sts

**Purl 1 row

K2, p2 to last 3 sts, k2, p1

P1, k2 *p2, k2, repeat to end

Purl 1 row**

Repeat from ** to ** for 8 in. (20cm)

With right side facing, decrease: k2, k2tog *k5, k2tog repeat to last 3 sts, k3

Work 4 rows in rib (k1, p1) to end

Cast off

To make back legs (x2)

Work as for front legs, repeating from ** to ** for 10 in. (25cm).

Sew side seams together on wrong side. Weave in the loose ends and turn the right way out

cutesy booties

Just like their tandem humans, some dogs have delicate feet—sensitive to cold tiles, scratchy lawns, or any surface that's not luxurious shag-pile carpeting. Why not knit your pet a set of booties to ensure those precious paws are kept coddled and warm—or bandages safe from curious gnaws?

These are for a small dog with 2 in. (5cm) paws and an ankle circumference of 3.3 in. (8.5cm). They can easily be adjusted to fit a larger dog by using size 9 (5.5mm) needles with chunky yarn or made smaller with size 6 (4mm) needles and double knit yarn.

MATERIALS

Size 7 (4.5mm) knitting needles
Aran yarn
Darning needle

DIRECTIONS

Make four

Cast on 24 sts

K1, p1 to end of row

P1, k1 to end of row

K1, p1 to end of row

P1, k1 to end of row

Work the next 20 rows in garter stitch

**On the first 6 sts only, continue in garter stitch, working 10 more rows

With right side facing, k1, k2tog, k1 turn, k to end of row

K2, k2tog, k1

Pick up 6 sts down side of heel and knit to the other side of the bootie**

With wrong side facing, repeat from ** to **

With right side facing, k9, k2tog, k10, k2tog, k9

Knit 1 row

K8, k2tog, k10, k2tog, k8

Knit 1 row—28 sts

Knit 8 more rows

Shape front: k6 * k2tog, k1, k2tog, k6, repeat from *

Knit 1 row—24 sts

K5, k2tog, k1, k2tog, k4, k2tog, k1, k2tog, k5

Knit 1 row—20 sts

K4, k2tog, k1, k2tog, k2, k2tog, k2, k2tog, k4

Knit 1 row—16 sts

Cast off and weave in the ends

On the wrong side, fold in half
and match the edges. Sew from
middle of toe section to edge and
back to toe for reinforcement.
Repeat on the other side

From the middle of the toe section,
continue to sew up the back of the
foot and leg to the top. Weave in
the ends and turn to the right side

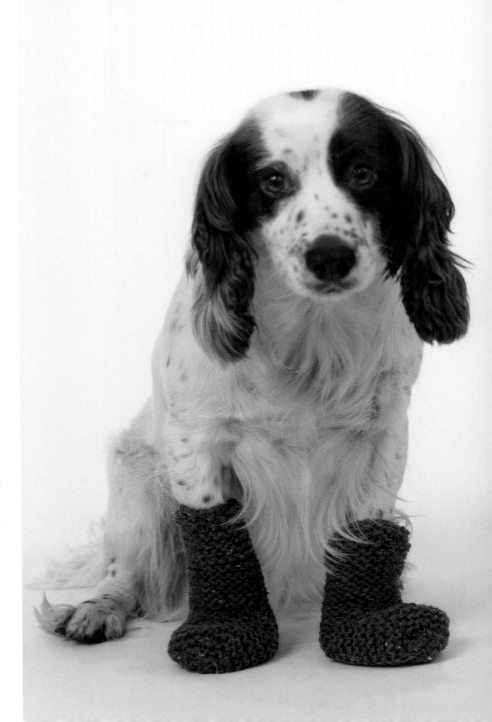

sports fanatic bobble hat

Cute worn solo as a quirky beanie, but even better paired with a corresponding scarf (see pp. 34–35), this pattern can be customized to the colors of your favorite sports team or alma mater. So put Percy's barking at the TV to good use, as he helps you reprimand your team's bad play on game night.

When switching between colors, it is easier to cut and rejoin the yarns as needed. This set was made for Tilly the spaniel, who has a span of 4 in. (10cm) between her ears. For a larger dog, try using chunky yarn and larger needles.

MATERIALS

Double knit yarn in black (or chosen color)
Double knit yarn in yellow (or chosen color)
Size 6 (4mm) knitting needles
Darning needle
Store-bought or handmade pompom (turn to pp. 48–49 for instructions on how to make them)
Elasticized band (optional)

DIRECTIONS

Using black yarn, cast on 84 sts
Work first 6 rows in rib (k1, p1)
Switch to yellow yarn, work 6 rows in rib
Changing back to black, work 6 rows in rib
Continue in yellow, work 6 rows in rib
In black, work 2 rows in rib
Decrease: k1, p1, * k3tog, p1, k1, p1, repeat from * to last 4 sts, k3tog, p1. You should now have 56 sts
K1, p1 to end. Work 2 rows in rib
Switch to yellow. Work 2 rows in rib

Decrease: k1, p1, *K3tog, p1, k1, p1, repeat from * to last 6 sts,
k3tog, p1, k1, p1. You should now have 38 sts
Work 2 rows in rib
Switch to black and work 2 rows in rib
Decrease: k1, p1, *K3tog, p1, k1, p1, repeat from * to end. You should now have 26 sts
Work last row in rib
Cast off and weave in loose ends

Cut a 3 ft. (1m) length of yarn and
weave it through all stitches with
the sewing needle. Fasten on
the wrong side and sew the side
seam using loose ends where
you changed color to sew in
matching yarns
Stitch on the pompom
If desired, measure out and sew
on elasticized band to fit under
the chin

sports fanatic scarf

On its own: a lovely patterned winter scarf. But when paired with the sports fanatic bobble hat (see pp. 32–33) on game night, no ref calls will ever be safe again.

When changing yarn colors, it is easier to cut and rejoin them as needed. This scarf can easily be made to fit a smaller or larger dog—simply decrease or increase by four stitches for every inch you want to change. Shorten or lengthen as necessary.

MATERIALS

Size 6 (4mm) knitting needles
Double knit yarn in green (or chosen color)
Double knit yarn in white (or chosen color)
Darning needle

DIRECTIONS

Using green yarn, cast on
    30 stitches
Rib stitch (k1, p1) first 6 rows
Switching to white yarn, rib
    6 rows
Continue in alternate colors
    every 6 rows in rib until scarf
    measures 25 in. (65.3cm), or
    your desired length
Cast off and weave in loose ends

(Note: When dressing your dog in a scarf, always remember safety first. The scarf should be kept short enough so as not to catch underfoot. Ensure every dog in a scarf is supervised.)

feelin' fancy bowtie

Supper is in the oven, the wine has been decanted, lit candles flicker . . . The makings of a glorious dinner party are underway—but what's that? Winston's chewed collar doesn't quite match your glittering tiara? Make sure your four-pawed pal feels part of the proceedings with a dapper bowtie. Easy-on, easy-off, the feelin' fancy bowtie is just as fitting for a swanky soiree as it is for a daytime promenade.

When switching between colors, it is easier to cut and rejoin the yarns as needed. Alternatively, a single-color or self-striping yarn is adorable in its simplicity.

MATERIALS

Size 6 (4mm) knitting needles
Double knit yarn in blue (or chosen color)
Double knit yarn in orange (or chosen color)
Darning needle
Elasticized band (optional)

DIRECTIONS

With blue yarn, cast on 6 sts (S) (10 sts (M), 14 sts (L)
Knit 1 row
Purl 1 row
Switch to orange yarn and knit 1 row
Purl 1 row
Switch back to blue for 2 rows
Continue in this way until piece measures 7.5 in. (19cm), (8.7 in. (22cm), or 9.8 in. (25cm)
Cast off and weave in any loose ends
Using blue yarn, cast on 3 stitches (4sts, 5sts)

Work in stockinette stitch, incorporating stripes as done previously, until piece measures 1.6 in. (4cm), 2 in. (5cm), or 2.4 in. (6cm)
Cast off and weave in ends
Fold the larger length in half with knit side outward and sew in place
Wrap the small strip around the middle and secure at the back
Either loop through your dog's tag or measure out and sew on an elasticized band to fit around the neck

personalized doggie blanket

If you share your life (read: couch and bed) with a dog, chances are you'll have experienced waking up ice-cold in the middle of the night to find your precious pooch warm and snuggled in a nest of your blankets. Now you can make Fido his very own, with the gift of this cozy doggie blanket! And why not personalize it with his name, so there's no mistaking (see pp. 90–92)!

MATERIALS

Size 10½ (6mm) knitting needles
Chunky yarn in your dog's favorite
    color
Darning needle

DIRECTIONS

Cast on 84 sts
Garter stitch (knit each row) for
    first 7 rows to make a border
**K6, p72, then knit the last 6 sts
Knit 1 row**
Repeat from ** to ** until work
    measures 11 in. (28cm) from top
    edge of border
Garter stitch 6 rows to finish the
    border
Cast off and weave in any ends

cold
weather

chunky scarf for the larger dog

Smartly dressed Ruby looks set to tackle anything winter throws her way in this beautifully fringed, chunky scarf. Jack Frost, you've met your match.

This scarf can easily be made to fit a smaller dog; simply decrease by four stitches for every inch you want to change. Shorten as necessary.

MATERIALS

Size 10 (6mm) knitting needles
Double knit yarn in blue (or chosen color)
Darning needle
Contrasting double knit yarns in fuchsia, blue, and purple (or chosen colors)
Scissors

DIRECTIONS

Using blue yarn and holding two strands together, cast on 10 sts
Rather than knitting with two balls of yarn, reach into the hole at the top of the yarn ball to find the other end
*K1, p1 * repeat to end of row
*P1, k1 * repeat to end of row
Rows 1 and 2 together create a rib pattern. For all following odd rows, repeat row 1, and for all even rows, row 2
Knit in rib pattern until scarf measures 51 in. (129cm)
Cast off knit-wise and weave in the ends

To add fringing

Cut strands of contrasting colored yarn to 3 in. (7.5cm) lengths (it doesn't matter if they're not perfect, you can trim them later)
Start at the cast-on end of the scarf
Fold one fringe strand in half and feed the looped end through the first cast-on stitch, leaving the two cut ends on the other side
Pass the two cut ends through the loop and pull to tighten
Tie a small overhand knot at the top of the fringe to prevent it from loosening

Continue in this way, using different colors, along each cast-on stitch. Repeat for cast-off stitches so that both ends are fringed

Once all fringes are attached to scarf, trim the edges to the same length

(Note: When dressing your dog in a scarf, always remember safety first. The scarf should be kept short enough so as not to catch underfoot. Ensure every dog in a scarf is supervised.)

trendy cowl

Gorgeous, toasty, and *so* in vogue—ensure your pup is ahead of the fashion pack with this cozy cowl. Style it with your choice of buttons and yarn colors for a garment that is utterly unique. Pair it with legwarmers (see pp. 28–29) for couture cold weather loungewear that is sure to rival any Paris *dogwalk*.

This was made for Jade the grayhound, who has a neck circumference of 15 in. (38cm). To size it up or down according to your dog, reduce four stitches for every inch you wish to adjust. The pattern will work over this repeat of stitches.

MATERIALS

Size 10½ (6.5mm) knitting needles
Chunky yarn in pink (or chosen color)
Stitch markers
4 buttons
Sewing needle
Darning needle

DIRECTIONS

This cowl is worked from the top down. Markers are placed between each ribbed side to make it easier to separate the bands from the textured pattern

Cast on 46 sts

Work the first 4 rows in rib (k1, p1)

This is where the front bands and the main textured part are separated. You can use store-bought stitch markers or make them from scrap yarn by taking a 19 in. (50cm) length and tying it into a loop

Rib 5 sts, place a marker, knit 56 sts, place a marker, and rib the last 5 sts to the end of the row. These last 5 sts are for the buttonhole band

Make the buttonhole where stipulated. Rib 2 sts, cast off 2 sts, and rib remaining stitch. Turn and, continuing in pattern as set, cast on 2 sts where they had previously been cast off to complete the buttonhole and ensure the correct number of stitches in the row

**Rib 5 sts, slip marker, knit to next marker, slip marker, rib 5 sts to finish row

Rib 5 sts, slip marker, purl to next marker, slip marker, rib 5 sts to finish row

Rib 5 sts, k2, p2 to marker, slip
  marker, rib 5 sts to finish row
On these first 5 sts, work a
  buttonhole. P2, k2 to marker, slip
  marker, rib 5 sts to finish row**
Repeat from ** to ** for 26 more
  rows, making the buttonhole
  every 4th row
Cast off, weave in all loose ends,
  and sew on buttons

chic shawl

This stylish shawl is the supreme in poochie panache. Fabulously versatile, it's a winner for dressy dos and sofa slacking alike. Perfectly paired with a matching French beret (see pp. 22–23), novice knitters will love this simple project.

This shawl was made for a dog with a neck circumference of 13.4 in. (34cm). To make it fit a smaller pet, stop increasing at a lower number or continue increasing to adjust it to a larger one. It should tie loosely around the neck.

MATERIALS

Size 10½ (6.5mm) knitting needles
Double knit yarn in blue (or chosen color)
Darning needle

DIRECTIONS

Cast on 3 sts
Knit 1 row
M1, k1, m1
Knit 1 row
**M1, knit to last stitch, m1
Knit 1 row**
Repeat from ** to ** until you have 83 sts
Cast off and weave in the ends

pompom scarf
for petite pooches

Stylish, warm, *and* fun! What diminutive cutie wouldn't love this bright and cheerful pompom scarf for crisp fall days?

This scarf can easily be made to fit a larger dog; simply increase by four stitches for every inch you want to change. Lengthen as necessary.

MATERIALS

Size 3 (3.25mm) knitting needles
Multicolored double knit yarn
Contrasting double knit red yarn
  (or chosen color)
Darning needle
Scissors

DIRECTIONS

Cast on 30 sts
Work in stockinette stitch until
  scarf measures 10 in. (25cm)
Cast off
With purl side facing outward,
  fold the scarf lengthwise and
  sew along the long edge to
  create a tube
Turn the scarf the right way out so
  the knit side is on the outside and
  sew along the end seams, keeping
  the long back seam running
  straight down the middle
To create the loop, fold one end
  back on itself (on the seamed
  side) by 2 in. (5.5cm) and sew it
  in place. Then pass the other
  end of the scarf through
  the loop, ready to attach the
  pompom to the end

To make a pompom

If you have a pompom maker, you can
  use it here. If not, pompoms are easy
  to make by hand
Leaving a strand loose, wrap
  the red yarn around four fingers
  of your free hand at least
  40 times. (The more times
  you wrap it around, the thicker
  the pompom)
Carefully remove the yarn from
  your fingers and tightly wrap
  the yarn around the center of
  this bundle five or six times.
  Tie tightly with the loose strand
  to secure it
With your scissors, cut all the
  loops and trim the ends to
  create an even, round shape
Sew onto the end of the scarf

(Note: When dressing your dog in a scarf, always remember safety first. The loop should be kept loose and the scarf short enough so as not to catch underfoot. Ensure any dog in a scarf is supervised.)

adorable sweaters

simple roll-neck pullover

A wonderful pattern for newer knitters looking to craft their first sweater, this simple roll-neck is also amazingly snuggly. And if your dog is short on legs but long on walks, he'll appreciate the cozy knit protecting his belly from snowy sidewalks. Choose single colors, self-striping yarn, or your choice of personalized lettering (see pp. 90–92) to create a charming pullover that truly is one of a kind.

MATERIALS

Size 7 (4.5mm) knitting needles
Size 5 (3.75mm) knitting needles
Double knit yarn in green (or chosen color)
Contrasting yarn in white (for optional lettering)
Darning needle

All dogs are different shapes and sizes, so instead of giving you S, M, and L options to follow, this pattern allows you to design a bespoke sweater that fits your pooch perfectly.

Before getting started, measure your dog and do some quick calculations.

First, check your dog's neck and chest (behind the front legs and up around the body) circumferences, as well as back length (from the collar to where you'd like the sweater to end). Multiply the neck and chest measurements by 5 to gauge the number of stitches needed.

The example measurements below are Casper the Jack Russell's:

Neck: 12 in. (31cm)–60 sts

Chest: 16 in. (41cm)–80 sts

Length: 14.5 in. (37cm)

Knit the sweater from tail to neck in two pieces. Dividing the stitches between the front and back is up to you; a ratio of ¼ for the front and ¾ for the back works well. With 80 sts in total as Casper's chest circumference, I used 60 sts for the back (Back Chest—BC), leaving 20 for the front (Front Chest—FC).

Make the front piece as one long rectangle without increases or decreases; the front chest and neck widths are the same:

Front piece: Chest, 20 sts (FC)— Neck, 20 sts (FN)

The decreases leading up to the neck are created in the back piece. To figure out the number of stitches for the neck on the back piece, take the total number of stitches for the neck circumference (e.g., 60 sts for Casper) and subtract the Front Neck. Writing all the stitches down before you start will help.

Back piece: Chest, 60 sts (BC)— Neck, 40 sts (BN)

See overleaf for directions

DIRECTIONS

To make back piece

With size 5 needles, cast on BC stitches

Work in rib (k1, p1) for 8 rows

Switching to size 7 needles, knit across one row, then purl the next row

If you wish to incorporate letters into the back of the sweater, do so in this section

The decrease toward the neck is created by k2tog (or p2tog, depending on which side you are on) at the end of each row, so there is a decrease of 2 sts every row. Figure out the difference between Back Chest and Back Neck (e.g., 20 sts for Casper) and divide this by 2. This is how many rows it will take to reach your desired number of neck stitches. Using the gauge 3 rows = 0.4 in. (1 cm), divide the number of decrease rows by 3 to figure out how many centimeters you must allow for it. Call this decrease measurement DM

Work in stockinette stitch until piece measures the total required length minus DM, ending with a purl row

**k1, k2tog, knit to last 3 sts, k2tog, k1

P1, p2tog, purl to last 3 sts, p2tog, p1**

Repeat from ** to ** until BN number of stitches remain

Switch to size 5 needles and work in rib (k1,p1) until ribbed section measures 5 in. (12.7cm)

Cast off and weave in any loose ends

To make front piece

Using size 5 needles, cast on FC stitches

Work in rib for 8 rows

Switching to size 7 needles, knit one row across

Purl the next row

Continue in stockinette stitch until front piece measures total required length

Switching to size 5 needles, work in rib until ribbed section measures 5 in. (12.7cm)

Cast off and weave in any loose ends

With your sewing needle and green yarn, sew front and back together along the edges, leaving spaces for the leg openings

stylish stripes sweater

A great pattern for intermediate knitters, the self-striping yarn does all the work in this adorable sweater so you don't have to! Ensure you measure accurately so it can fit over your little darling's head, but once this knit's on, she'll feel so snug, she won't want it to come off. And neither will you, once those compliments start pouring in . . .

All dogs are different shapes and sizes, so instead of giving you S, M, and L options to follow, this pattern allows you to design a bespoke pullover that fits your pooch perfectly.

Before getting started, measure your dog and do some quick calculations.

First, check your dog's neck and chest (behind the front legs and up around the body) circumferences, as well as back length (from the collar to where you'd like the sweater to end). Multiply the neck and chest measurements by 5 to gauge the number of stitches needed.

The example measurements below are Poppy the Yorkshire terrier's:

Neck: 10 in. (25cm)–50 stitches

Chest: 18 in. (46cm)–90 stitches

Desired length: 15.5 in. (39cm)

Use a circular needle from neck to tail. If the neck stitches are too few to fit on a circular needle, start with double-pointed needles (DPNs) and switch when there are enough.

See overleaf for directions

MATERIALS

Size 6 (4mm) circular knitting needle
Size 6 (4mm) double-pointed needles
  (DPNs)
Self-striping double knit yarn
Contrasting double knit yarn in cream
  (or chosen color)
Round marker
Stitch holder
Darning needle

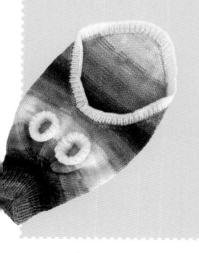

DIRECTIONS

Using DPNs and self-striping yarn, cast on neck stitches (e.g., 50 sts for Poppy)

Set marker for beginning of round and work in rib (k1, p1) until piece measures 2.5 in. (6cm)

Switching to circular needle, knit every stitch across round

Knit 2 more rounds

Increase: After every increase round, write down the new number of stitches so you can keep track

M1, knit to end of row

M2, knit to end of row

M4, knit to end of row

M1, k6, m1, knit to end of row

M1, k1 5 times, knit to end of row

M1, k13, m1, knit to end of row

M1, k1 4 times, k1, **m1, k1** 4 times, knit to end of row

At this point, you should have increased by 25 sts. If you have reached your required number of stitches for the chest measurement, stop here and move on to **leg openings**. If not, continue to increase until you reach required amount

M1, k23, m1, knit to end of row

M1, k25, m1, knit to end of row

M1, k27, m1, knit to end of row

M1, k29, m1, knit to end of row

M1, k31, m1, knit to end of row

M1, k33, m1, knit to end of row

And so on . . .

To make leg openings

A V-shape should have appeared in the chest from the increases. At the bottom edges of this V, mark the points where you will cast off stitches to create leg openings. Count the stitches between the V (the same as the number of increased stitches), subtract 10 (these are to go between the two front legs), and divide by 2; giving you ___ sts

At beginning of next round, cast off ___ sts, k10, then cast off ___ sts again; this should take you to the other outside edge of the V

Knit to the end of the row, then put the 10 sts (for between the legs) onto a stitch holder

If your dog wears a harness, an optional opening can be made here for the leash attachment

(Count the number of stitches you are working on, subtract 6, then divide by 2 to get ___ sts)

Purl ___ sts, cast off 6 sts, then purl to end of row

Knit ___ sts, cast on 6 sts, then knit to end of row

Work in stockinette stitch for 12 rows, then cut yarn and put these worked stitches aside

Return to 10 sts on holder and knit 12 rows in stockinette stitch

Ending with a knit row, cast 8 sts onto the right needle, knit across the stitches on the holder, cast on 8 sts to right needle again, then place marker for beginning of row

Continue knitting in the round for 12 rows

At beginning of next round, cast off 8 sts

**K1, k2tog, knit to last 3 sts, k2tog, k1

Turn and p1, p2tog, purl to last 3 sts, p2tog, p1**

Repeat from ** to ** until piece measures desired length (allowing 1 in./3cm for ribbed trim)

Note: If you wish to decrease slower, i.e. you want a longer back length, only decrease on the knit rows

Once piece is at desired length, keeping remaining stitches on needle, pick up all stitches along bottom edge of sweater

Using contrasting cream yarn, knit in rib (k1, p1) until ribbed trim measures 1 in. (3cm)

Cast off and weave in all loose ends

Using DPNs, pick up all stitches around leg opening

Place marker

Using contrasting cream yarn, knit every stitch for 1 round

Work 8 rounds in rib

Cast off all stitches, then roll back ribbed trim (you might need to sew it in place)

Repeat for other leg opening

preppy puppy letterman sweater

MATERIALS

Size 3 (3.25mm) knitting needles

Size 6 (4mm) double-pointed knitting needles (DPNs)

Size 6 (4mm) circular knitting needle

Double knit yarn in maroon (or chosen color)

Contrasting yarn in gold (or chosen color)

Round marker

Stitch holder

Darning needle

Whether chewing over library books or chasing the neighbor's football, your pooch will look sufficiently collegiate in his varsity duds. With all that running, fetching, and chasing, you know he's earned his letter. (See p. 91 for old-school varsity lettering or choose a more unusual lettering style on pp. 90 and 93.)

All dogs are different shapes and sizes, so instead of giving you S, M, and L options to follow, this pattern allows you to design a bespoke pullover that fits your pooch perfectly.

Before getting started, measure your dog and do some quick calculations.

First, check their chest circumference (behind the front legs and up around the body), as well as back length (from the collar to where you'd like the sweater to end). Multiply the chest measurement by 5 to gauge the number of stitches needed.

The example measurements below are Percy the pug's:

Chest: 20 in. (51cm)—100 sts

Length: 12 in. (31cm)

See overleaf for directions

DIRECTIONS

This sweater is knitted from neck to tail

Using maroon yarn and size 3 knitting needles, cast on chest stitches (e.g., 100 sts for Percy)

Work in rib (k1, p1), decreasing 1 stitch at the edge of each row 16 times, which gives an overall decrease of 32 sts

Work 1 row in rib

Continuing in rib, m1 at each end of next 5 rows

Using gold yarn, m1, work in rib to end of row, m1. Repeat

Switching to maroon yarn, m1, work in rib to end of row, m1. Repeat

Switching to gold yarn, m1, work in rib to end of row, m1. Repeat

Work 5 more rows in maroon yarn, continuing with the increases to return to original number of chest stitches

Fold the ribbed V-neck at the middle with the double-striped side facing. Using the circular needle, knit the stitches on the needle together with the corresponding cast-on stitches opposite. You might find it easier to first pick up the cast-on stitches with the size 3 needle, then hold both needles alongside each other as you knit from these two onto the circular needle

Once all stitches are on the circular needle, set marker and knit 10 rounds

If you wish to knit your pet's initial onto the front, do so here with gold yarn. If not, knit 10 more rounds

K10 before the marker, cast off 2 sts, k8, remove marker, k8, cast off 2 sts, then knit to end

Transfer the 16 sts that are between the cast-off stitches to the stitch holder

If your dog wears a harness, an optional opening can be made here for the leash attachment

(Count the number of stitches you are working on, subtract 6, then divide by 2 to get ___ sts)

Purl ___ sts, cast off 6 sts, then purl to end of row

Knit ___ sts, cast on 6 sts, then knit to end of row

Work 26 rows

Cut yarn and return to 16 sts on holder

Work 26 rows

On next knit row, k16, then knit across back stitches and set marker here

Continue knitting in the round for 10 rows

At beginning of next round, cast off 16 sts, **k1, k2tog, knit to last 3 sts, k2tog, k1

Turn work and p1, p2tog, purl to last 3 sts, p2tog, p1**

Repeat from ** to ** until piece measures desired length (allowing 2 in./5cm for ribbed trim). If you wish to decrease slower because you want a longer back length, only decrease on the knit rows

Keep remaining stitches on needle and pick up all stitches at the bottom edge of the sweater

Using maroon yarn, knit in rib for 2 rounds

Switch to gold yarn and knit in rib for 2 rounds

Return to maroon yarn for 2 more rounds in rib

Cast off

Using DPNs, pick up all stitches around leg opening

Using maroon yarn, knit in rib for
3 rounds
Cast off using gold yarn to create
contrasting edging
Repeat for other leg opening
With maroon yarn, sew the V-neck
closed at the front. Weave in all
loose ends

holiday sweater

Why should humans have all the fun with outrageous holiday knitwear? This season, why not create a delightful sweater for your canine companion! And for added festive cheer, pair it with a charming elf hat (see pp. 20–21). With your faithful friend so well-dressed, this may be the year to relegate your own light-up Rudolph sweatshirt to the white elephant list.

All dogs are different shapes and sizes, so instead of giving you S, M, and L options to follow, this pattern allows you to design a bespoke pullover that fits your pooch perfectly.

Before getting started, measure your dog and do some quick calculations.

First, check your dog's neck and chest (behind the front legs and up around the body) circumferences, as well as back length (from the collar to where you'd like the sweater to end). Multiply the neck and chest measurements by 5 to gauge the number of stitches needed.

The example measurements below are Ivy the pug's:

Neck: 13 in. (33cm)–65 sts

Chest: 21 in. (53cm)–105 sts

Desired length: 14 in. (36cm)

Before starting, calculate the difference between the neck and chest stitches (e.g., 105 – 65 = 40 sts for Ivy) and call this "i"; this is the number of stitches you will need to increase by to reach the correct chest size.

Use a circular needle from neck to tail. If the neck stitches are too few to fit on a circular needle, start with double-pointed needles (DPNs) and switch when there are enough.

See overleaf for directions

MATERIALS

Size 6 (4mm) double-pointed needles (DPNs)
Size 6 (4mm) circular needle
Double knit yarn in red, green, white, and gold (or chosen colors)
Round marker
Stitch holder
Darning needle

DIRECTIONS

Using red yarn and circular needle (or DPNs), cast on neck stitches (e.g., 65 sts for Ivy)

Set marker for beginning of round and work in rib (k1, p1) for 10 rows

At beginning of next round **m1, k3**

Repeat from ** to ** to end of round

Make a note of the amount of stitches you have just increased by. You can subtract this amount from i to calculate the number of stitches you still need to increase by

Pick up green yarn and, continuing in stockinette stitch, start working in Pattern 1. It is worked as a repeat across 6 stitches. If the number of stitches on your needle isn't divisible by 6, increase stitches evenly across the row until you reach a divisible figure. Again, note the number of increased stitches and subtract this from i

At the start of row 9 in Pattern 1 (white row), **k3, m1, k2 **repeat to end of round. Again, make a note of the amount of stitches you have just increased by and subtract from i

Work to the end of Pattern 1

On the first row of Pattern 2 (green row), increase evenly throughout the row, all remaining increase stitches

While continuing work in Pattern 2, at beginning of next row, cast off 5 sts (for leg openings), k8 (for between the legs), cast off 5 sts again, then knit to end of row. If you wish to include a small opening for a leash to harness attachment, cast off 5 sts halfway through remaining stitches and cast them back on during the next row, like a buttonhole

Put the 8 sts between the leg openings on a stitch holder and work in Pattern 2

At the end of Pattern 2, cut yarn and return to 8 sts on holder

Work in green yarn for 19 rows

At the end of the next knit row, cast on 5 sts (over leg opening), knit across the back, cast on 5 sts, place marker here. All stitches should be on circular needle so work can continue in the round

Now work straight through Pattern 3 with no increases or decreases

At the beginning of Pattern 4 (red row), cast off 8 sts, then knit to end of row

Now work as you would on straight needles, backward and forward, turning the work at the end of every row

While continuing work in Pattern 4, **k1, k2tog, knit to last 3 sts, k2tog, k1

Purl 1 row**

Repeat from ** to ** until piece measures desired length (allow 1 in./3cm for ribbed edge)

For a faster decrease, if you're running out of length, p1, p2tog, p to last 3 sts, p2tog, p1, for the purl rows

Keeping remaining stitches on the needle, pick up all stitches along bottom edge and knit in rib (k1, p1) for 1 in. (3cm)

Cast off all stitches

Using DPNs, pick up stitches around leg openings and knit in rib for 6 rows

Cast off and weave in the ends

Fold the ribbed neck in and sew it in place with red yarn

urban hoodie

Just imagine being the littlest pup on the block, with everyone bossing you around. What you need is to stand out, take charge, claim your own patch of delicious turf. And what better way than with a hand-knit urban hoodie, complete with your own stitched "tag" across the back? It's instant street cred to tackle the suburban wilderness.

MATERIALS

Size 6 (4mm) double-pointed knitting needles (DPNs)
Size 6 (4mm) circular knitting needle
Double knit yarn in blue (or chosen color)
Contrasting double knit yarns in black and white (or chosen colors)
Round marker
Stitch holder
Darning needle

All dogs are different shapes and sizes, so instead of giving you S, M, and L options to follow, this pattern allows you to design a bespoke pullover that fits your pooch perfectly.

Before getting started, measure your dog and do some quick calculations.

First, check your dog's neck and chest (behind the front legs and up around the body) circumferences, as well as back length (from the collar to where you'd like the sweater to end). Multiply the neck and chest measurements by 5 to gauge the number of stitches needed.

The example measurements below are P Dawg's (Percy the pug's):

Neck: 13 in. (33cm)–64 stitches

Chest: 20 in. (51cm)–100 stitches

Desired length: 12 in. (30.5cm)

Using a circular needle, knit from neck to tail. If the neck stitches are too few to fit on a circular needle, start with DPNs and switch when there are enough.

See overleaf for directions

DIRECTIONS

Using main color, cast on neck stitches (e.g., 64 sts for Percy)

Set marker for beginning of the round and work in stockinette stitch in the round for 6 rows

Increase: at the beginning of the row m2, knit to end of round

M1, k2, m1, knit to end of row

M1, k4, m1, knit to end of row

M1, k6, m1, knit to end of row

M1, k8, m1, knit to end of row

M1, k10, m1, knit to end of row

Continue in this way (increasing the knit stitches between the increase stitches by multiples of 2) until you have the desired number of stitches for the chest measurement (e.g., 100 sts for Percy)

A V-shape should have appeared in the chest from the increases. At the bottom edges of this V, mark the points where you will cast off stitches to create leg openings. Count the stitches between the V (the same as the number of increased stitches), subtract 14 (these to go between the two front legs), and divide by 2, giving you ___ sts

On the next round, when you reach the first edge of the V, cast off ___ sts, k14, then cast off ___ sts again. This should take you to the other outside edge of the V

Transfer the 14 sts (for between the legs) to a stitch holder and knit to the end of the row

If your dog wears a harness, an opening can be made here for the leash attachment

(Count the number of stitches you are working on, subtract 6, then divide by 2 to get ___ sts)

Purl ___ sts, cast off 6 sts, then purl to end of row

Knit ___ sts, cast on 6 sts, then knit to end of row

Work in stockinette stitch for 15 rows (if you wish to add letters from the Urban Alphabet, on p. 90, do so here) then cut yarn and put these worked stitches aside

Return to 14 sts on holder and knit 15 rows in stockinette stitch

Ending with a knit row, cast 10 sts on to the right needle,

knit across the stitches on the holder, cast on 10 sts onto right needle, then place marker for beginning of row

Continue knitting in the round for 18 rows

At beginning of next round, cast off 14 sts, k1, k2tog, knit to last 3 sts, k2tog, k1

Turn and p1, p2tog, purl to last 3 sts, p2tog, p1

**K1, k2tog, knit to last 3 sts, k2tog, k1

P1, p2tog, purl to last 3 sts, p2tog, p1**

Repeat from ** to ** until piece measures desired length (allowing 1.5 in./4cm for ribbed trim)

If you wish to decrease slower, i.e. you want a longer back length, only decrease on the knit rows

Keeping remaining stitches on circular needle, pick up all stitches along bottom edge of sweater

Set round marker, then knit one round using contrasting black yarn

Work 3 rounds in rib (k1, p1)

Using contrasting white yarn, work 2 rounds in rib

Switch back to black yarn and work
3 more rounds in rib
Cast off

Using DPNs, pick up all stitches
around leg openings
Place marker and knit 1 round in
contrasting black yarn
Work 2 rounds in rib
Switch to white yarn and work
2 rounds in rib
Using black again, work 2 rounds
in rib
Cast off

Hood
Pick up all stitches along right side
of neck from middle at the front
to middle at the back
With knit side facing, knit 1 row
Turn and purl next row
Continue in stockinette stitch until
rectangle measures 6 in. (15cm)
Cast off all stitches
Pick up all remaining neck stitches
along left side of neck
With knit side facing, knit 1 row
Turn and purl next row
Continue in stockinette stitch until
rectangle measures 6 in. (15cm)
Cast off and weave in any edges
Using blue yarn, sew along the back
and top edges of hood

costumes

superhero cape and wristbands

Is it a bird? Is it a plane? No, it's Super Coco! Hardly faster than a speeding bullet or able to leap tall buildings in a single bound, but dressed in his flashy Wonder Woman-style cape and wristbands, your pup will be aptly attired for patrolling the house for villains—*ahem*, uninvited guests.

This pattern was created for Coco the bulldog, who has the following measurements:

length of back: 18 in. (46cm); chest (circumference behind armpits at the front): 28 in. (72cm); neck circumference: 22 in. (57cm). Should you wish to create this item for a smaller dog (with a girth of around 8–10 in./20–22cm), try using a lighter-weight yarn, such as Aran, and size 9–10 (5.5–6mm) needles. Created according to the sizing above, the item should fit dogs of a similar size, and the neck can be taken in if necessary and the belt tightened. However, if you'd like more of a custom fit, this pattern is best for an advanced knitter able to extrapolate from the bespoke pattern sizing above.

See overleaf for directions

MATERIALS

Size 10½ (6.5mm) knitting needles
Chunky yarn in blue (or chosen color)
Chunky yarn in yellow (or chosen color)
Chunky yarn in red (or chosen color)
2 stitch holders
Darning needle
Crochet needle

DIRECTIONS

Cast on 62 sts in blue yarn and rib (k1, p1) for 1.5 in. (4cm)

Work 12 rows in stockinette stitch

To divide for armpits, k6, and put these stitches on a stitch holder

Cast off 7 sts. This forms the beginning of an armpit

Knit 36 sts and place on a stitch holder. These stitches are going across the back of the dog

Cast off 7 sts for second armpit, knit 6 to end

Knit 7 rows of stockinette stitch across these 6 sts and place on stitch holder

Put 36 sts back on needle and work 7 rows of stockinette stitch. Place back on stitch holder

Place 6 sts back on needle and knit 7 rows in stockinette stitch.

Turn. K6, cast on 7 sts, k36 from stitch holder, cast on 7 sts, k6 from stitch holder

Now work along the back. You have a choice here as to how far down the back you want the coat to go and where you introduce the "belt"

Work 6 rows in stockinette stitch, decreasing 1 stitch at each end of knit row—56 sts

Work 12 rows in stockinette stitch, decreasing 1 stitch at end of every row—44 sts

Change to yellow yarn, knit to end, and cast on 25 sts to form the belt. The blue edging is added afterward

Purl next row in yellow yarn

K3 in yellow, change to red, knit to last 3 sts, k3 in yellow

P3 in yellow, change to red, purl to last 3 sts, p3 in yellow

Knit 3 in yellow, change to red, k to last 3 sts, k3 in yellow

Work 2 more rows in stocking stitch with yellow yarn

Cast off the edge of the belt and continue to work up the coat in blue, decreasing 1 stitch at the end of every row over 16 rows

Cast off remaining stitches

Stitch up seam under belly

With blue yarn, crochet double-crochet stitches all around the outside of garment and around the front leg holes

To make "cape"

With yellow yarn, pick up 40 sts over upper edge of neckline, where rib meets stockinette stitch

Knit in garter stitch for 10 rows, increasing 1 stitch at end of every row

Work 10 more rows in garter stitch, decreasing a stitch at end of every row

Cast off

Crochet edge around the yellow cape

To make wristbands (x2 or 4)

For front legs, cast on 13 sts, work in blue yarn and rib (k1, p1) for 3 rows

Knit in alternating colored stripes until desired length

For back legs, work as front legs over 15 stitches

Join seams and weave in all ends

bumblebee

Delicately fluttering through the air, it's Carla the nimble-footed bulldog! Ideal for a fancy-dress party or a good gallivant through the daisies, this bumblebee outfit is soft and warm, with dainty fine-spun wings that rise and fall with each graceful leap.

This pattern was created for Carla the bulldog puppy, who has the following measurements:

neck circumference: 18 in. (46cm); width around at foreleg front (armpit): 9 in. (23cm); width from foreleg to back leg along the belly 13 in. (32cm). Should you wish to create this item for a smaller dog (with a girth of around 8–10 in./20–22cm), try using a lighter-weight yarn, such as Aran, and size 9–10 (5.5–6mm) needles. Created according to the measurements above, the item should fit dogs of a similar size. However, if you'd like more of a custom fit, this pattern is best for an advanced knitter able to extrapolate from the bespoke pattern sizing above.

MATERIALS

Size 13 (9mm) knitting needles
Size 8 (5mm) knitting needles
Merino yarn in black
Merino yarn in yellow
Bergère de France Éclair yarn in Neige
Darning needle

DIRECTIONS

To make body
With black yarn and size 13 needles, cast on 34 sts
Work in k2, p2 rib for 6 rows
Increase stripe: switch to yellow yarn
**Knit 4 rows
K2, m1, knit to last 2 sts, m1, k2
Knit 1 row**

Repeat from ** to ** 5 more times, alternating between black and yellow yarn
Knit 6 rows in yellow yarn
Knit 6 rows in black yarn
Repeat last 12 rows twice more, or until desired length
Cast off

To make underside
Using black yarn and size 13 needles, cast on 18 sts

Work in k2, p2 rib for 6 rows
Knit 6 rows in yellow yarn
Knit 6 rows in black yarn
Repeat last 12 rows 3 more times
    or until desired length
Cast off

To make wings (x2)
Using Neige yarn held double
    and size 8 needles, cast on 8 sts
Knit 2 rows
K2, yo (wrap yarn around right
    needle), k4, yo, k2
Knit 3 rows
*K2, yo, * repeat 4 times, k2
Knit 3 rows
K2, yo, k3, yo, k4, yo, k3, yo, k2
Knit 3 rows
K2, yo, k3, yo, k3, yo, k2, yo, k3, yo,
    k3, yo, k2
Knit 3 rows
K2, yo, k2tog (knit 2 together),
    k1, yo, k2tog, k1, k2tog, yo, k4,
    yo, k2tog, k1, k2tog, yo, k1, k2tog,
    yo, k2
Knit 3 rows
K2, yo, k2tog, k1, yo, k2tog, k2tog,
    yo, k1, k2tog, k2tog, k1, yo, k2tog,
    k2tog, yo, k1, k2tog, yo, k2
Knit 3 rows
K1, k2tog, yo, k2, k2tog, yo, k2,
    k2tog, k2tog, k2, yo, k2tog, k2,
    yo, k2tog, k2, yo, k2tog, k1
Knit 3 rows

K1, k2tog, yo, k1, k2tog, yo, (k2tog
    4 times), yo, k2tog, k1, yo k2tog, k1
Knit 3 rows
K1, k2tog, yo, k1, k2tog, yo,
    k2tog, k2tog, yo, k2tog, k1,
    yo, k2tog, k1
Knit 3 rows
K1, k2tog, yo, k1, k2tog, k2, k2tog,
    k1, yo, k2tog, k1

Knit 3 rows
Cast off
Join upper and lower body and,
    starting at cast-on edges, sew for
    3 in. (8cm). Leave 4.5 in. (12cm)
    gaps for the leg opening, and sew
    remainder of the seam
Sew wings to the top center of the
    body. Weave in all ends

Elizabethan ruff

You know your little madam thinks she's queen, so why not play along and let her dress the part? With similarly attired cohorts including Queen Elizabeth I and William Shakespeare, she'll be in fabulous company (although *their* collars didn't attach to practical harnesses for everyday use—at least, not that we know of!).

Before starting, measure your dog's neck circumference in centimeters (to convert inches to centimeters, multiply by 0.3937008). Multiply this figure by 2, and then by 4. For example, a neck measurement of 13.8 in. works out at 35cm; multiplied by 2, is 70 stitches, and again by 4 is 280 stitches. This total figure is the amount of stitches you will need to cast on.

MATERIALS

Size 6 (4mm) circular needle
Double knit yarn in white (or chosen color)
Contrasting double knit yarns in gray and navy blue (or chosen colors)
Sewing needle
Spare fabric harness or collar

DIRECTIONS

Using blue yarn, cast on necessary amount of stitches

Working in the round, place marker, then knit 1 row

Purl 1 row

Using gray yarn, knit 1 row

Switch to white yarn and knit 10 rows

K2tog across entire round, then repeat for next row

Knit 1 round

At beginning of round, turn work and knit stitch across all the purl stitches

M1 across the entire round, then repeat for next row

Knit 12 rows

Using gray yarn, knit 1 row

Switch to blue yarn and knit 1 row

Purl 1 row

Cast off all stitches

Fold ruff along the middle, making sure the longer half is sitting underneath and knit side is facing up. Sew onto harness or collar

rabbit-ear bonnet

Could that pitter-patter and soft snuffling be the Easter Bunny? No, dear, it's Percy Pug in his delightful rabbit-ear bonnet, on the hunt for all those hidden treats. But beware . . . come Easter morning, you may just end up with a basketful of wrappers.

MATERIALS

Size 10 (6mm) knitting needles
Size 7 (4.5mm) knitting needles
Double knit yarn in white (or chosen color)
Sirdar Snuggly Snowflake yarn in shade 0703 (or chosen color)
Darning needle

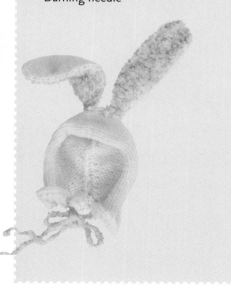

DIRECTIONS

To make bonnet sides (x2)
These make up the sides of bonnet and are knit from bottom to top
Holding two strands of white yarn together, cast on 12 sts
**Knit to last 2 sts, m1, k1
Purl 1 row**
Repeat from ** to ** until there are 18 sts
Knit 12 rows in stockinette stitch
**Knit to last 3 sts, k2tog, k1
Purl 1 row**
Repeat from ** to ** until 10 sts remain
With knit side facing, match pieces together and sew along the back and top to create hood shape, then turn the right way out

To make ruffle trim
Pick up all stitches along bottom of bonnet
With knit side facing, knit one row across
Purl 1 row
M1 into every stitch
Purl 1 row
M1 into every stitch
Cast off

To make ears (x2)
Using double knit white yarn and holding two strands together, cast on 4 sts
Knit 1 row
Purl 1 row
K2, m1, k1
Work 3 rows in stockinette stitch
K2, m1, k2
Purl 1 row

K3, m1, k2

Purl 1 row

K3, m1, k3

Purl 1 row

K4, m1, k3

Purl 1 row

K4, m1, k4

Purl 1 row

Knit 22 rows in stockinette stitch

K1, K2tog, knit to last 3 sts, k2tog, k1

P1, P2tog, purl to last 3 sts, p2tog, p1

Cast off and weave in any ends

Using Snowflake yarn and size 7 (4.5mm) needles, repeat above steps for making inside of ears

Don't worry if the fluffy ears look smaller than the white; the yarn is very stretchy once it is knit and will fit!

Place one white ear against one fluffy ear with purl sides facing and sew along the edges using white yarn. Repeat with the other ear

Sew both ears to the bonnet

For ties (x2)

Cut six strands of Snowflake yarn to required length

Holding three strands together, tie a knot at one end

Braid strands together, finishing with a knot at the other end

Repeat with the other three strands, then sew into the bottom edges of the bonnet

cupcake skirt

Cute as a button, this cupcake skirt and matching frosting bonnet are so ridiculously adorable, we could just eat them up! Dress up your dainty darling in this ensemble for Halloween to get trick-or-treaters cooing at your door.

This outfit is suitable for a pet with a "waist" measurement of 14–16 in. (35–41cm). To adjust the size, you can decrease or increase the number of stitches by four per inch of difference.

Use smaller needles and thinner yarn for a smaller dog or larger needles and thicker yarn for a bigger dog.

MATERIALS

Size 6 (4mm) knitting needles
Double knit yarn in color A
Double knit yarn in color B
Buttons and beads
Elastic thread in color A (optional)
Darning needle
Sewing needle

DIRECTIONS

To make cupcake case skirt

Cast on 96 sts in color A

Use rib stitch (k1, p1), adding in the increased stitches as purls on the wrong side (odd rows), and knits on the right side (even rows). You can include the elastic thread with your yarn as you knit or you can sew it in at the end. It will help with the fit

For first 6 rows, *ktbl (knit into the back of the stitch), p1* to end of row

Increase 8 sts evenly across row by m1 on 8 knit sts to 104 sts

For next 5 rows, repeat from * to *
Repeat from ** to ** to 112 sts
For next 7 rows, repeat from * to *
Repeat from ** to ** to 120 sts
For next 3 rows, repeat from * to *

For the fluted edges

On first 10 sts, *k2tog (knit 2 together), k6, K2tog, turn, p2tog, p4, p2tog, turn, k2tog, k2, k2tog, turn, cast off 4 sts*

Rejoin yarn to the next 10 sts and repeat from * to * to end of row

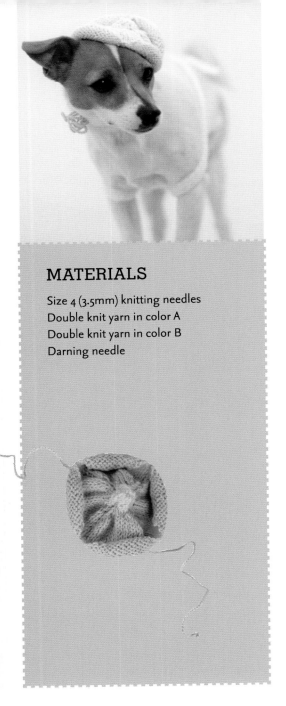

frosting bonnet

This is for a small dog with a span of 4 in. (10cm) between the ears. It is knitted in four sections that are then sewn together. An additional "petal" can be added for a slightly larger dog, but any more than this may flatten the shape. Using chunky yarn and larger needles would ensure a fit for a medium to large dog.

DIRECTIONS

Make four

With color A, cast on 2 sts
Knit 1 row
Purl 1 row
M1, m1
Purl 1 row
M1, k2, m1
Purl 1 row
M1, k4, m1
Purl 1 row
M1, k6, m1
Purl 1 row
M1, k8, m1
Purl 1 row
M1, k10, m1
Purl 1 row
M1, k12, m1
Purl 1 row—16 sts
Mark the beginning of this row with a thread to be used later and knit 1 row
Stockinette stitch for 10 rows

With right side facing, decrease k2tog (knit 2 together), k2tog, k8, k2tog, k2tog
P2tog (purl 2 together), purl to last 2 sts, p2tog—10 sts
K2tog, k2tog, k2, k2tog, k2tog
P2tg, p2, p2tog—4 sts
Now join color B
Knit 1 row
Purl 1 row
K2tog, k2tog
Purl 1 row
Cast off

To make ties (x2)

Cast on 30 sts, then cast off 30 sts
On wrong side, using yarn in color A, sew edges of "petals" together from the marker thread to the top. Remove the marker threads. Sew over the top of the petals to close. Attach ties to two adjacent petals, so they can be tied on either side of the head. Weave in ends

MATERIALS

Size 4 (3.5mm) knitting needles
Double knit yarn in color A
Double knit yarn in color B
Darning needle

To make frosting for cupcake case skirt

With the inside of the cupcake case facing, pick up 120 sts along the last row before the fluted edges. Turn with right side facing, join color B, and knit to end of row

Work next 5 rows in stockinette stitch

K2tog, * k9, k2tog * continue to end of row, knitting any additional stitches

Work next 3 rows in stockinette stitch

K2tog, * k8, k2tog * continue to end of row, knitting any additional stitches

Work next 3 rows in stockinette stitch

K2tog, * k7, k2tog * continue to end of row, knitting any additional stitches

Work next 3 rows in stockinette stitch

K2tog, * K6, K2tog * continue to end of row, knitting any additional stitches

Cast off and weave in the ends

Embellish with buttons or beads

Sew side seam of the case, leaving the frosting open

Sew fluted edges to the frosting to ensure it lays flat

To make straps (x2)

These can be adjusted to fit. The straps should cross at the middle of the back, loop over the shoulder, and attach to the middle of the waist

Cast on 7 sts and work in rib (k1, p1) until the strap measures 13.5 in. (34cm)

For buttonhole, rib 3, cast off 1 stitch, rib to end of row

Rib to end of row, cast on 1 stitch to replace cast-off stitch

Continue ribbing for a further 1.5 in. (4cm). Cast off and weave in the ends

Stitch straps to the back of the cupcake case, cross over, and add buttons underneath to secure

templates

The horizontal rows represent the rows you will knit on your needle, and each square represents a stitch. As you move along the row, change the yarn color accordingly. Note: Each square represents a stitch on your row. Remember, if you are knitting a sweater from bottom to top, start at the bottom of the chart so that it doesn't come out upside down!

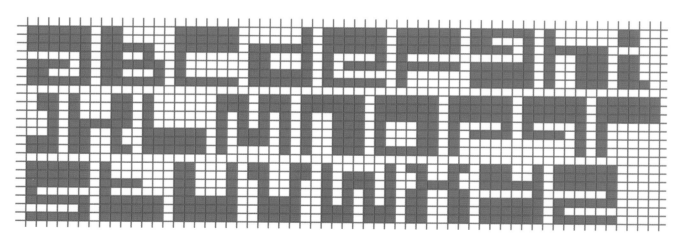

URBAN ALPHABET

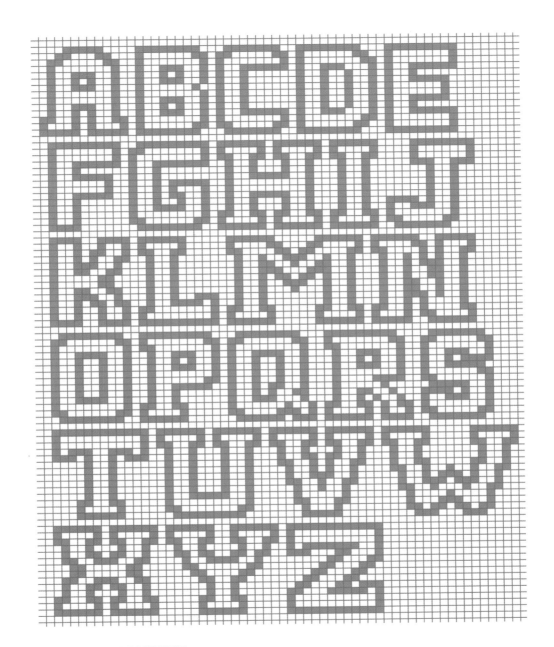

VARSITY ALPHABET

PREPPY PUPPY ALPHABET

OUTRAGEOUSLY ADORABLE DOG KNITS

CHRISTMAS PATTERN CHART

contributors

Caitlin Doyle (writer/editor) is half-writer/half-editor, half-American/half-British. Caitlin learned to knit from her nana and mother (but previously plateaued at scarves) and has been newly inspired by these lovely knitters to try her hand at creating fetching sweaters and accessories for Ivy, her do-anything-for-a-treat pug. Caitlin has written and edited a number of books for adults and children for over 15 years, but *Outrageously Adorable Dog Knits* remains one of her most cherished.

Jill Bulgan (knitter) has been knitting for 48 years, since first starting at 4 years of age. Jill is a Scot married to a Turk living in London, England, with three children and one grandchild. Jill is never *not* knitting (even on the bus!). You can find her on www.ravelry.com as "Knit with Jill." Jill loves all forms of crafting, and she is currently pursuing patchwork and quilting. She hopes to write her own knitting book in the near future. Jill is dedicated to passing on to the next generation her knowledge and knitting skills.

Noelle Woosley (knitter) is a young actress from South London, England, and the proud owner of Percy the Pug. When it came to the matter of dressing him, she struggled with sizing; hence, she learned to knit in order to provide bespoke, comfortable pieces for him. If you would like a handmade piece for your dog or are having trouble with any patterns in the book, you can contact her via the "Bespoke Doggy Knitwear by Noelle" Facebook page.

Rachael Matthews (knitter) is an artist and author, with a primary interest in knitting. Born in the Lake District in England, she grew up with an interest in textile traditions and romanticism. The founder of Cast Off Knitting Club for Boys and Girls, she was a pioneer in the new wave of KIP and the author of two books that illustrated the movement, *Knitorama* and *Hookorama*. Rachael uses knitting and crochet as sculpture and painting, and knitted garments are illustrations for stories. Rachael runs Prick Your Finger, an ethical yarn shop and textile gallery in East London, which sources fibers and handspins its own yarns.

Max Alexander (knitter) started designing and making jewelry for knitters in 2009. Max loves knitting, and the designs sprang out of a desire to wear something wooly, even when it was too warm for knitwear. In 2011, Max made the knitted knitting octopus, which featured in many craft blogs. Max also makes large knitted sculptures and knitted stop-motion animations (knitimations), winning Best Animation at The National Student Film Festival in 2007 and 2008, as well as Best Music Video in 2008.

Claire Lloyd Davies (photographer) is a lifestyle photographer living in Hampton, England, with Tilly, her cocker spaniel. Claire studied photography at Rochester Institute of Technology in New York and Salisbury Art College in England. A woman who loves a challenge, Claire has made a living out of breaking the rule of never working with children or animals. She travels internationally for her work on a range of magazines and books and can be contacted through her website at www.clairedavies.com, where some examples of her other work can be found.

Gemma Birss (craft writer) has mixed up a juicy cocktail of careers as an air hostess, artist, film maker, and radio DJ. Having lived in Iran, Zimbabwe, South Africa, Japan, India, and France, she is now settled in the UK, where she writes, edits, knits, and draws. Yarn-hunting is her hobby, and she has been known to crochet slightly impractical garments from the innards of her old cassette tapes.

acknowledgments

The biggest appreciation goes to all the lovely dog models and their equally lovely owners for their involvement in this project. So huge gratitude to the Davies-Stockley family (and Tilly), Kirsten Rose (and Poppy), Noelle Woosley (and Percy), Hannah Cohen (and Ruby), the Cooper-Firth family (and Jade), Jo Brignall (and Casper), Chi-Bun Cheng (and Elmo), Mario Crisan (and Coco and Carla), Ivy, and Adam Grieve (Schnitzel and Harry ⌐
to the incredible knitters, w
some downright bizarre re
and make them look fabu⌐

Thank you to everyone who allowed their homes to be turned into doggie studios for the day, including the Davies-Stockley family and three Doyle households. Sorry for all the dog hair. Thanks to the HarperCollins Rights team for boundless enthusiasm for this project. Much appreciation goes to Jacqui Caulton for her beautiful design and to Claire Davies for her hilarious and stunning images and work as co-dog wrangler.
⌐Northcote Road, for the loan of
l with dogs. Finally, credit
sharing a subjectively